PUBLIC SPEAKING MADE EASY

Manage Your Nerves, Engage with Ease,
and Deliver Your Message with Maximum Impact

PUBLIC SPEAKING MADE EASY
Manage Your Nerves, Engage with Ease,
and Deliver Your Message with Maximum Impact

Copyright © 2017 by Dominic Mann

All rights reserved. This book or any portion thereof may not be reproduced or used in any manner whatsoever without the express written permission of the publisher except for the use of brief quotations in a book review.

PUBLIC SPEAKING MADE EASY

Manage Your Nerves, Engage with Ease,
and Deliver Your Message with Maximum Impact

By
Dominic Mann

TABLE OF CONTENTS

Introduction 5
Nonverbal Communication 7
   Speaking Without Words: The Key to a Powerful Presence 7
   Body Language 8
   How to Develop a Powerful Presence with Powerful Body Language ... 9
   Gestures 12
   Voice 14
   Master Your Nonverbals to Influence How Your Audience Feels and Their Perception of You 20
Ethos, Pathos, Logos 22
   Aristotle's Guide to Rhetoric 22
How to Structure Your Speech 25
   Structure 25
   The First 30 Seconds: The Most Important Part of Your Speech 25
   Tell Them What You're Going to Tell Them: How to Introduce What You're Talking About in a Unique and Engaging Way 28
   Body: Tell Them 31
   Conclusion: Tell Them What You Told Them 35
Storytelling 37
3 Steps to Becoming the Most Charismatic Person in the Room ... 39
How to Prepare to Give the Speech of Your Life 41
   5 Steps to Preparing the Perfect Speech 41
   The 10/20/30 Formula for the Perfect Presentation 43
   How to Quickly and Efficiently Memorize Your Speech from Start to Finish 45
Conclusion 51

INTRODUCTION

People judge books by their covers.

You can be the most skilled, accomplished, and talented person at your company or in your industry, but if you lack charisma, confidence, and the ability to speak in a convincing and engaging manner, none of that will matter.

When it comes to people's perceptions of you, confidence equals competence. The confident and charismatic public speaker will be perceived by others to be more credible and competent than someone who's shy and awkward yet who may actually be more skilled.

Yes, this is a little sad and unfair, but it's just the way the human mind works. Appearances matter and the ability to present yourself to others and speak in public very often wins the day.

Don't believe me? Then read on...

Research by the Carnegie Institute of Technology examined the major factors that contribute to one's financial success. What did they find? Their research shows that 85 percent of a person's financial success is due to their ability to lead, negotiate, and communicate—all of which is related either directly or indirectly to your public speaking abilities. Shockingly, only a measly 15 percent of your financial success is due to your technical knowledge.

Put simply, when it comes to your financial success, your ability to communicate with and present yourself to others is more than six times more important than skill, talent, or intellect. *It's really that important.*

But it doesn't end there.

In most lines of work, public speaking is an essential part of securing business. Whether it be making your case at an important meeting, winning over clients, or pitching investors, public speaking plays a crucial role in determining your success.

Clearly, public speaking is important. But what you might be missing is *just how important it is.* You're not going to dominate meetings, conquer presentations, win over clients, or have investors signing checks simply by smiling and putting encouraging facts and figures on a PowerPoint slide.

No. You need to win them over emotionally as well as logically. You need to captivate, charm, and make them fall in love with you.

A study by Nobel Prize winning psychologist Daniel Kahneman found that—rather shockingly—people prefer to do business with those they like and trust (as opposed to those they don't)… *even if the likable person offers lower quality products/services at a higher price!*

Yes. You read that right. Become a charismatic speaker and you can woo over investors, board members, clients, and more, *even if your competitors are offering a better product or service at a lower price!*

That is the power of effective public speaking.

And if you want to find out how you can develop this incredible power and put it to work in your own life for jaw-dropping results, then read on…

In the first chapter, you'll learn how to develop an awe-inspiring presence and speak volumes before you even so much as open your mouth…

NONVERBAL COMMUNICATION

SPEAKING WITHOUT WORDS: THE KEY TO A POWERFUL PRESENCE

"Hey!" a man angrily shouts at you, aggressively waving his fist in the air.

"Hey!" says your aunt as she greets you in the doorway for Thanksgiving.

"Hey," says a guy/girl flirtily, giving you a wink.

Words can mean all sorts of different things. Real communication is done through gestures, body language, tone of voice, eye contact, posture, and other nonverbal cues.

Some scientific studies have gone so far as to conclude that only seven percent of communication is done through actual words. The other 93 percent comes from body language (55 percent) and tone of voice (38 percent).

While this particular study may place a little too much emphasis on nonverbal communication, the point still stands: your nonverbals are an important (if not *the* most important) part of your ability to communicate. This is especially true when it comes to public speaking.

If you want engage, captivate, and charm your audience, mastering nonverbal communication is essential. If you want to develop irresistible charisma, mastering your nonverbals is essential. If you want to cultivate an authoritative, powerful presence, mastering... well, you get the idea.

It all comes down to your nonverbals. And for good reason, too. Long before us humans began to use spoken language as a way to communicate, we relied purely on nonverbal cues.

Is that wolf making angry eye contact with ears flattened and teeth bared while growling? Probably a good idea to stay away from it. In evolutionary times, our ancestors would have made similar judgements, based on nonverbal cues, about fellow cavemen. As a result, us humans are absolute masters of picking up on subtle nonverbal cues. Ever met somebody and got a "bad feeling" about them? That's your subconscious picking up on the subtlest of nonverbal cues.

And when it comes to public speaking, you can either use the extraordinary power of nonverbal communicate to your advantage or to your detriment. To learn how to do the former, read on…

Lesson: When it comes to how other people perceive you, your nonverbals are everything.

BODY LANGUAGE

How do you use your body? What does your posture look like? Do you stand tall with chin up, chest out, and shoulders back? Or do you slouch over, walk in little, quick steps, and keep your eyes down?

Do you move slowly and deliberately with confidence? Or do you move in quick, jerky movements, as if nervous or unsure of yourself?

The way you move your body says a lot about you. The way you move your body also makes a distinct impression on those around you. It's the difference between someone who comes across as nervous and awkward, and someone who comes across as authoritative, powerful, and confident.

So then… how can you use your body language to develop a powerful presence that commands respect… and not an awkward, nervous presence that inspires only pity?

Read on to find out…

Lesson: Your body language can be the difference between appearing confident and sure of yourself or timid and uncertain.

HOW TO DEVELOP A POWERFUL PRESENCE WITH POWERFUL BODY LANGUAGE

Imagine an executive in his office. He's leaning back into his chair, feet up on his desk, hands clasped behind his head with elbows out.

How do you think he feels? If his body language is anything to go by, he's feeling pretty good about himself. If someone were to stroll into his office, they'd get the distinct impression that he's a very confident guy.

Now, let's imagine the opposite. Imagine a lowly employee, or perhaps someone applying for an unimportant job. They're seated in a chair. They're leaning forward, slouching a little. Their hands are in their lap, their feet are crossed under the chair. They're rocking back and forth a little bit and often look down, struggling to hold eye contact for long.

What sort of impression does this guy's body language give you? Clearly, he's nervous, perhaps a little intimidated. He gives the impression of lacking confidence and is probably unsure of himself and a little uncomfortable. Put simply, he's definitely *not* confident.

So what is it that makes the "vibe" that these two people give off so different? Why does one come across as supremely confident and authoritative, while the other comes across as meek and uncertain? It all comes down to the following...

The Body Language Spectrum

On one side of this spectrum, you have body language that exudes power and confidence. On the other, you have body language that screams timidity and awkwardness. Here are the two sides of the spectrum:

- **Open and expansive body language—taking up lots of space.** Imagine someone with their legs spread wide apart, leaning back, with one arm resting on the back of a chair next to them. This type of body language gives the impression of confidence and power.
- **Closed and constricted body language—shrinking your body language and taking up as little space as possible.** Imagine somebody with arms crossed or hands in their lap, eyes averted and looking at the ground, hunched over, with jerky, uncontrolled movements. This type of body language gives the impression of shyness and weakness.

This is crucial to public speaking. If you want people to have confidence in your message, you must *appear* confident. And when you appear confident, people will also perceive you to be more competent and more credible (regardless of whether or not this perception matches reality).

That said, your body language affects more than just your audience. Your body language also affects *you*...

Lesson: If you want to look confident, then take up lots of space, stand tall with your chest out, etc. If you want to look timid, take up as little space as possible, cross your legs and arms, hunch over and look down at your feet, etc.

How to Feel More Confident and Relaxed W Speaking to an Audience

Studies have found that when your body language is closed and constricted (taking up as little space as possible) your body releases cortisol, the stress hormone. When you make your body language open and expansive (taking up lots of space), however, your body releases testosterone, a hormone associated with confidence and power.

In other words, when you *act* confident, you actually *become* confident. Conversely, when you act intimidated, uncertain, or shy, you begin to feel as such.

For a more in depth explanation of this effect and the studies behind its discovery, take a look at Amy Cuddy's TED talk, *Your Body Language Shapes Who You Are*. (Watch it here: https://www.ted.com/talks/amy_cuddy_your_body_language_shapes_who_you_are.) The talk has over 50 million views as of this writing (including the video on YouTube).

In addition to the aforementioned study, Amy Cuddy and other researchers conducted another similar experiment testing how job interviews could be impacted by doing a two-minute "high power pose" beforehand. A "high power pose" is basically posing using supremely confident body language, such as standing in a victory pose (as if you've just crossed the finish line of a marathon and have pumped your fists into the air as a display of victory). Cuddy says that before a high-stakes situation, such as a job interview or speech, this could be done in a private space such as a bathroom stall, so you don't look like a lunatic doing these odd poses for minutes at a time.

So what were the study's results? What was the impact of doing a "high power pose" before a job interview?

The results were clear: those who did a two-minute "high power pose" before a job interview performed better across the board, made better impressions, and were significantly more likely to be hired.

Lesson: With confident body language, you'll not only *look* confident and powerful, you will begin to feel as such. Conversely, with weak, submissive body language, you'll begin to feel nervous and timid.

GESTURES

Whereas your body language gives people an overall feeling or impression of you (are you confident and authoritative, or weak and timid?), hand gestures are much more specific. Gestures can be used to emphasize something, call attention to a specific detail, or to help your audience comprehend what you're saying.

While there are many different types of gestures—many of which are entirely spontaneous—you can divide most into three main categories: gestures that are symbolic, descriptive, and for emphasis. Let's take a closer look at each...

Symbolic Gestures

Symbolic gestures are quite specific. They can be used to communicate specific words, numbers, positions, and more. Here are some examples:

- **Listing.** For example, using your fingers to list your points: "My first point is X, my second point is Y, and my third point is Z." You could also use three fingers to say something like, "There were three bananas."
- **Pointing.** You can point (or gesture using your whole hand) to communicate certain positions, such as up, down, behind, beside, etc.

- **Universal, specific gestures.** For example, a thumbs up for agreement or a raised hand for a stop.

Descriptive Gestures

Descriptive gestures communicate a more general idea, size, or movement. For example:

- **Size.** "It was *this* big." Or spreading your hands to communicate that something was big or long. Similarly, you could communicate that something is very small by holding your thumb and index finger (or your hands) close to together.
- **Shape.** You can use your hands to show a shape.
- **Movement or flow.** You can sway your hands to communicate movement.

Gesturing for Emphasis

You can also use your hands to emphasize certain points or ideas. Think of this like underlining, *italics*, or highlighting. Here are some example gestures:

- **Pointing.** Even if you're not pointing at anything specific, gesturing with a pointed hand can be a powerful way to gesture. That said, it is a very strong gesture and should only be used if you're emphasizing something very important or serious. (President Obama used this gesture quite a bit. President Bill Clinton used this forceful gesture when denying he had an affair with Monica Lewinsky. Hitler also frequently used this gesture.)
- **Chopping.** Similar to the pointing gesture, chopping is another forceful gesture that should only be used appropriately. You do it by using your hand to "chop" the air. For even more emphasis,

you can chop onto the palm of your other hand. (Al Gore sometimes used this chopping gesture.)
- **Upward-facing palm.** This is a less forceful, much more friendly gesture. You do it by gesturing with your hand with your palm facing upward. This is probably the best and most common way of gesturing and emphasizing specific points. Having your palm facing upwards also makes you appear much more friendly, agreeable, and warm. Unless you're emphasising something very important or serious, this gesture is usually the best way to go.
- **Downward-facing palm.** Similar to chopping and pointing, gesturing with your palm facing downward is a more forceful, demanding, authoritative gesture. Use only when that is the impression you want to make. (For example, think of the Nazi salute—an undoubtedly forceful and authoritative-looking gesture.)

Moving on, let's take a look at the final aspect of nonverbal communication…

VOICE

Let's say I were to have you listen to two audio clips in a language you don't understand. One clip would be of Hitler giving one of his rousing speeches, and another would be of a German comedian doing stand up comedy.

Even without understanding what they're saying, the two audio clips would give you very different impressions.

Why?

You have no clue what they're saying. You can't even see their body language or hand gestures.

The reason you get distinctly different impressions from each is because of the way they use their voice. Hitler is going to be shouting and using his voice in an incredibly dramatic way. The stand up comic is going to be talking in a more relaxed, conversational manner, perhaps altering his voice in a humorous way when delivering a punchline.

Although it may not seem like it, the way you use your voice can have a big impact on your audience. It can be the difference between boring them or captivating them. You can put your audience to sleep by speaking in a monotone, or you can put them on the edge of their seats by raising your voice, lowering your voice, pausing, emphasising certain words, and so on.

Read on to find out more about specific ways you can use your voice to engage, captivate, and charm…

Inflection

Inflection (or intonation, or voice modulation) is perhaps the most obvious way that the way you use your voice can influence the meaning of what you're saying. Basically, inflection is when you change the pitch or tone of your voice.

A common example of inflection is when we ask a question. For example, say aloud the following question: "The car was stolen?" Because it's a question, you would have raised the pitch of your voice slightly at the end of the question.

Now, say the same thing, but do *not* raise your voice at the end. You get this: "The car was stolen." It's a statement, not a question. When we're speaking, though, the only way we know the difference is because of the upward inflection (or the lack thereof) at the end of the sentence.

But inflection can be used to communicate a lot more than just a question mark. For example, you might speak louder to express excitement, or softer to communicate sadness. Inflection can also be used to emphasise specific words, and, in the process, change the entire meaning of what you're saying.

Read on to take a look at the different ways inflection can be used to emphasize, engage, and keep your audience awake…

- **Upward inflection.** This is when your voice goes from a lower pitch to a higher pitch within the vowel. This can indicate a question, surprise, insincerity, etc. Say the following words and raise the pitch of your voice at the end: "Really", "No!" "Wow!" Consider the difference in meaning without the inflection (or with a downward inflection instead).
- **Downward inflection.** This is the opposite of an upward inflection—instead of raising the pitch of your voice within the vowel, you lower the pitch of your voice. Downward inflections communicate decisiveness, certainty, confidence, finality, power, authority, etc. Say the following words and lower the pitch of your voice toward the end: "Go", "No", "Done". Consider how the downward inflection influences what these words convey.
- **Level inflection.** In other words, no inflection. The pitch of your voice does not change within the vowel. This can indicate indecision or disinterest. Say the following examples without changing the pitch of your voice: "Fine", "OK", "Maybe".
- **Circumflex inflection.** This is when the pitch of your voice both rises *and* falls (up-down-up) or falls and then rises (down-up-down) within the vowel. Not sure what this sounds like? Try saying the following words in the manner described above: "Well", "Wow", "Please", "So", "Go", "Hey".

As you can see (or hear?), inflection can greatly influence the meaning of what you're saying. Lowering your inflection at the end of a sentence makes it sound more authoritative and declarative, whereas an upward inflection at the end of a sentence indicates the opposite—surprise, questioning, etc.

Perhaps most importantly (as this will probably be your most common application of it), you can use inflection in the middle of a sentence to emphasize something, make it more interesting, or bring attention to a specific detail or a point that you are making.

Here's a quick exercise for you that will underscore just how much impact inflection can have on the message you are conveying. Read the following sentences, putting an inflection on the bolded word

Sentence: "***I** didn't say she stole the stapler.*"
Likely Response: "*If you didn't say it, who did?*"

Sentence: "*I didn't **say** she stole the stapler.*"
Likely Response: "*So you wrote it?*"

Sentence: "*I didn't say **she** stole the stapler.*"
Likely Response: "*So someone else stole it?*"

Sentence: "*I didn't say she **stole** the stapler.*"
Likely Response: "*So she borrowed it? Or maybe it was a gift?*"

Sentence: "*I didn't say she stole the **stapler**.*"
Likely Response: "*So she stole the pencil sharpener?*"

Lesson: By adding an inflection to a specific word, you can completely change the meaning of what you're saying. You can also alter the feeling you give the audience (i.e. whether you come across as authoritative, conversational, questioning, excited, etc.). Skillfully incorporate inflection into your speech (but not excessively, or you'll just sound downright bizarre) and you'll have a more engaged audience.

Pause

Most people are terribly afraid of public speaking. As such, they memorize their speech (or just read off their slides) and try to get it done as quickly as possible. They try to rush through it without so much as a pause for breath.

Skilled public speakers know better. In addition to speaking in a slower and more controlled manner, they also frequently make use of pausing. President Obama, for example, was a huge fan of using pauses in his speeches to emphasize certain sentences or to let something he had said sink in.

Pausing can also have a powerful effect in a place you might not expect: the very beginning of your speech, before you say a single thing.

Most people get up to the lectern (or the front of the room, or from wherever you are delivering your speech) and begin talking immediately. Instead, try pausing for a moment. Just pausing, scanning the crowd, and standing in silence before your audience conveys an aura of confidence and authority. You can even pause long enough for people to start thinking something might be wrong. When you finally begin your speech after pausing for a while and scanning the audience, you can be certain you've already captured the audience's attention—without even saying a word.

Lesson: Pause, pause, pause. Pause to let your audience catch up. Pause to emphasize a specific point and give the audience time for it to sink in. Pause to let your audience think, "Yes, I agree with that!" Pause to build suspense (give your audience time to think, "What's coming next?"). Pause for humor (e.g. "Always remember that you're unique. ... *pause* ... Just like everyone else."). Pause after asking a question to give your audience a moment to think about it. Pause to separate different points, concepts, or ideas. And *really* pause. No, uhmms or ahhs. When speaking... pause.... Give people time to absorb what you're saying... to agree with you... to wonder what's coming next... to emphasize and separate points... and so on....

Pace and Projection

Two final factors that affect how your audience perceives you and what you have to say are pace and projection.

- **Pace.** How fast are you talking? Do you slow down to emphasize a particularly meaningful sentence? Do you manipulate your speaking pace to create energy and excitement?
- **Projection.** Are you speaking loud enough? Are you loud enough for everybody to hear, yet not to the point of sounding overbearing? Or are you too soft, making it difficult for people to hear and coming across as insecure or lacking confidence? Do you speak louder and softer when appropriate—for emphasis and emotional impact—to keep your audience engaged, captivated, and listening to your message?

Lesson: You can alter your pace and projection to give your words added impact and meaning. Skillfully manipulate your pace and projection while speaking and people will find themselves drawn into what you're saying.

MASTER YOUR NONVERBALS TO INFLUENCE HOW YOUR AUDIENCE FEELS AND THEIR PERCEPTION OF YOU

Skilled public speakers don't just communicate a message. They share a *feeling*.

Watch a wartime speech—such as from Churchill, Roosevelt, or Hitler—and you'll come away feeling fired up. Watch a speech by Martin Luther King during the civil rights movement or Barack Obama during 2008 and you'll come away feeling inspired. Watch a speech by Malcolm X and you'll come away feeling angry at injustice. Watch a pre-game speech by Muhammad Ali or a speech by John F. Kennedy, and you'll find yourself feeling motivated.

The thing people will remember most is not what you said, but how you made them *feel*. And the key to influencing how people feel lies in your nonverbals. The way you hold yourself (posture) and move your body. The way you gesture (e.g. forceful pointing and chopping gestures vs. relaxed palm-up gesturing). The way you use your voice (e.g. do you speak loudly and clearly, pause for effect, emphasize words with your pitch, etc.?).

The harsh truth (or perhaps good truth if you embrace it and use it to your advantage) is that the actual words that come out of your mouth matter very little. The overall impression and "feeling" people have of you and what you have to say is formed not by your words, but predominantly by your nonverbals.

Lesson: Your nonverbal communication, not your verbal communication, plays the biggest and most important role in determining how people perceive you and how they feel about your message.

Now that you've learned how to build a powerful presence that commands respect as well as how to use your body, hands, and voice to say so much more than mere words ever could, it's time to take a look at the foundation of rhetoric itself...

ETHOS, PATHOS, LOGOS

ARISTOTLE'S GUIDE TO RHETORIC

The ancient Greek philosopher Aristotle wrote a masterful guide to persuasive public speaking called *Rhetoric*. Aristotle's work is regarded by most rhetoricians as "the most important single work on persuasion ever written." It has also been said that "all subsequent rhetorical theory is but a series of responses to issues raised" by Aristotle's *Rhetoric*.

In *Rhetoric*, Aristotle outlines three different methods of persuasion:

1. **Ethos.** Ethos refers to attempting to persuade people by appealing to one's credibility. For example, a doctor rarely has any trouble "persuading" his or her patients to take a certain medication or course of action. You can apply this to your own speeches by referring to sources of credibility. For example, have you successfully done something like this before? Do you have a degree on this topic? Are you an industry expert? A professor or executive with inside knowledge on this particular topic?
2. **Pathos.** Pathos refers to appealing to the audience's emotions, such as by pointing out an injustice, eliciting sympathy, agreeing with values shared by the audience, etc. Pathos can also include appeals to hope (e.g. Obama's "Hope" slogan and speeches) or painting a picture of a positive future resulting from following the proposed cause of action (e.g. Martin Luther King's "I Have a Dream" speech). Pathos also includes appeals to fear and other negative emotions, for example Donald Trump frequently appealed to fear during his 2016 presidential campaign. Here is a

definition of "pathos" in Aristotle's words: "Secondly, persuasion may come through the hearers, when the speech stirs their emotions."
3. **Logos.** Logos refers to logic. For example, the statement, "All men are mortal, Socrates is a man, therefore Socrates is mortal," is rather convincing due to it's appeal to logic. Logos also includes referring to facts, figures, and other forms of evidence that back up your argument.

The use of ethos, pathos, and logos as rhetorical devices can be summarised as follows: before you can persuade an audience, they must first accept you as credible (ethos); your audience must then feel an emotional connection with you and/or your message, because people predominantly think and act based on emotion (pathos); finally, your argument should make sense and be backed up with facts and figures and other evidence.

Credibility. Feeling. Logic.

They must feel that you're an expert or a trustworthy source. They must feel some sort of emotion that tugs them in the direction you want (love, sympathy, hate, envy, fear, hope, etc.). And they must feel that your argument is based on logic and facts.

You may have noticed that I repeatedly used the word "feel." This is not a mistake. *Everything* comes down to the way your audience feels. Feeling, feeling, feeling.

Dodgy salesmen can make a quick buck by purporting themselves as a credible source, appealing to the buyers emotion (e.g. fear or hope), and making up (or exaggerating or misusing) facts. They can be slick and charming, making their victim *feel* as if they can trust them.

Lesson: When seeking to persuade an audience through your speech, make sure to incorporate references to your credibility, an emotional component, as well as references to facts, figures, and evidence.

HOW TO STRUCTURE YOUR SPEECH

STRUCTURE

Speech structures can vary from those that are downright utilitarian (no nonsense, hyper-logical, gets the job done) to those that have a little more creativity and artistic flair.

In this chapter, you'll learn the basic template that virtually all speeches should follow, all the ins and outs of different sections of your speech, as well as ways you can make your speech highly unique and add your own creative touch to make for an unforgettable speech.

Read on to learn how to structure your speech for maximum impact…

THE FIRST 30 SECONDS: THE MOST IMPORTANT PART OF YOUR SPEECH

The first thirty seconds (or in many cases, even less) of your speech are the most important. What you say during these crucial first moments will determine whether your listeners seat themselves on the edge of their seats, eager to hear what you have to say next, or zone out and wait for you to finish without really listening to what you have to say.

So… how can you get your audience engaged from the get-go? Here are some different ways you can do just that…

Attention Grabbers

Immediately grab your audience's attention and capture their interest with one of the following:

- Ask a thought-provoking question.
- Tell a story or anecdote.
- Make a startling statement or reveal an astonishing fact.
- Icebreaker—make a joke (risky as this may backfire) or a reference to the audience, occasion, previous speech, current events (especially within your industry), etc.
- Relevant quotation (and if you like to be bold, perhaps one that is controversial or shocking).
- Expert opinion or prediction (be careful with predictions though because if your prediction turns out to be wrong, this will hurt your credibility in the future).
- And more, so get creative. The "attention grabber" you use to open your speech may also depend on the purpose of your speech, who your audience is, or your industry. For a creative example, read on below…

A brilliant example of an attention grabber is from Dan Pink's TED talk: "The Puzzle of Motivation." (See the TED talk here: https://www.ted.com/talks/dan_pink_on_motivation/). He starts off his speech by saying the following:

"I need to make a confession at the outset here. A little over 20 years ago, I did something that I regret, something that I'm not particularly proud of. Something that, in many ways, I wish no one would ever know, but here I feel kind of obliged to reveal. (Audience laughter.) In the late 1980s, in a moment of youthful indiscretion, I went to law school. (Audience laughter.)"

Now, I don't know about you, but that sure grabbed my attention and got me eager to hear what he had to say next.

Moving on, let's now take a look at something else that can be important when starting a speech and making a good first impression with your audience…

SEE Factors

In direct marketing (e.g. door-to-door sales), you're taught to do two major things when you first start talking to someone you're pitching: icebreakers and SEE factors.

You break the ice by making a relevant joke, mentioning something about the surroundings, or just saying g'day and asking them how their day is.

Whereas breaking the ice has more to do with what you actually say, SEE factors have more to do with your nonverbal communication. "SEE" is an acronym: **s**mile, **e**ye contact, **e**xcitement (or **e**nthusiasm—after all, you don't want to look unenthusiastic about what you're selling).

While SEE factors is something taught in sales, it can also be applied to public speaking. Within those crucial first thirty seconds, you want to:

- **Smile.** Or at least look happy to be there, you don't necessarily need to grin like a fool. (Note: It is still important to be aware of your situation. For example, if you're giving a eulogy, it might not be very appropriate to give everyone a big grin.)
- **Make eye contact.** At the beginning of your speech, before you start, you can scan the audience. As you speak, you'll want to keep your eyes on the audience. Don't look at your feet, your notes, at the PowerPoint slide, or anything else. No. Always look

at the audience. If you're concerned about being distracted by people's faces, look slightly above people's heads or look at the back of the room.

- **Show excitement and enthusiasm.** If you don't care about what you've got to say, why should anybody else? Don't talk like a boring old university professor who's giving the same lecture for the 40th year in a row and boring his students brainless. Instead, speak with passion and vigor. (Once again, you need to be aware of your situation. Continuing the eulogy example, you'll want to show that you care about what you have to say not with excitement and enthusiasm, but perhaps with solemnness and admiration for the deceased's accomplishments, the way they lived their life, and those whose lives they've touched, etc.)

Your first thirty seconds are crucial. Within those thirty seconds (or less), you must grab your audience's attention, get them interested in what you have to say, and then make a smooth if not seamless transition into the rest of your speech.

Now that you've grabbed your audience's attention and made a favorable impression by smiling, making eye contact, and showing enthusiasm for what you're going to be talking to them about, let's take a look at what you should do next…

TELL THEM WHAT YOU'RE GOING TO TELL THEM: HOW TO INTRODUCE WHAT YOU'RE TALKING ABOUT IN A UNIQUE AND ENGAGING WAY

"Almost every guidebook for speech writing will say to choose your topic. It's an obvious starting place. But a lot of people miss out the fact that you need to also select the core message that you want to get across."

— Ryan McLean

Once you've deployed your attention grabber, you'll need to introduce the topic you're going to talk about (i.e. "tell them what you're going to tell them"). Ideally, you will incorporate this into your "attention grabber" in your first thirty seconds.

For example, if you're giving a talk about self-driving cars, you might start by telling a story about a friend of yours who was killed in a car accident when you were younger. You can then link this into what your speech will be about by telling the audience that this tragic event inspired you to want create a world in which what happened to your friend would not have happened through your work in the development of self-driving cars. Then, having got the audience's attention, you can then introduce what your speech is about by briefly outlining three reasons self-driving cars will make roads safer (or whatever the main points are that you will make in your speech).

Here is a brief, step-by-step guide for starting your speech in a powerful way:

1. **Pause.** Don't immediately start talking. Take a few moments to take a breath, scan the audience, and relax. This will get all eyes on you as well as give you an aura of confidence and power. Then, once your silence has got everybody's attention and all eyes are on you…
2. **Deploy your attention grabber.** Start with a story, controversial statement, a relevant quote, anecdote, etc. See above for a whole list of different attention grabbers. Make sure to relate your attention grabber to the topic of your speech and then…
3. **State the purpose of your speech.** Why should your audience care? How does it relate to them? Why are you speaking? What are you trying to accomplish with this speech? Let your audience know the purpose of your speech. Make them want to listen. State

your purpose very concisely with a single sentence. Don't waffle on. Then...

4. **Tell them what you're going to tell them.** What will your main points be? Succinctly state what you're going to tell them. For example, if you have three major points that you're going to expound upon in your speech, briefly state them.

Now remember, you need to do all of this quickly (though don't speak quickly). Be concise. You want your introduction to feel more like a surgeon's scalpel than a rusty axe.

It's simple:

Grab their attention with a quote, controversial statement, short story, or other attention grabber.

Tell them why you're there.

Tell them what you're going to tell them.

That's it. It should take no more than 30 seconds (unless you're giving a long speech).

Ken Robinson's TED talk: "Do Schools Kill Creativity?" gives us a great example of a solid introduction (See the TED talk here: http://www.ted.com/talks/ken_robinson_says_schools_kill_creativity/).

It's very simple, yet gets the job done.

Robinson **breaks the ice** by starting his speech in a very conversational way and getting a few laughs.

"Good morning. How are you? (Audience laughter.) It's been great, hasn't it? I've been blown away by the whole thing. In fact, I'm leaving. (Audience laughter.)"

He then **outlines the three main points** he is going to talk about.

"There have been three themes running through the conference which are relevant to what I want to talk about. One is the [...]. The second is that [...]. And the third part is that [...]."

He then finishes up his introduction by concisely **stating the purpose of his speech.**

"So I want to talk about education and I want to talk about creativity. My contention is that creativity now is as important in education as literacy, and we should treat it with the same status. (Audience applause.)"

It's really that simple.

BODY: TELL THEM

So you've grabbed their attention, told them what you're going to tell them by briefly outlining your main points, and you've told them the purpose of your speech.

Now what?

Now you just need to tell them.

Ask yourself: what is the purpose of your speech? What are you trying to do? Are you trying to convince? Persuade? Educate? Inspire action?

The way you structure your speech will depend a great deal on what it is you're trying to accomplish (i.e. the purpose of your speech).

That said, regardless of what you're discussing or what you're trying to accomplish, the body/middle of your speech will almost always need the following two things:

1. **The body of your speech will need to be organized around a few key points or main ideas.** You need structure. You can't just toss out random idea after random idea and try to bumble together a string of random thoughts. Limit your speech to three main ideas (or "key points", or "arguments", or whatever you want to call them). If your speech is a little on the longer side, you may be able to get away with five main ideas.
2. **The body of your speech will need signposting and transitions.** You need to make it abundantly clear that you're discussing your first point, or your second, or so on by signposting. Give your audience a helping hand and remind them of where they are in the speech. For example, you will want to say things like, "My first point is [X]," and "Moving on to my second point..." You will also need smooth transitions so your speech doesn't feel too clunky. Smooth it out with transitions that express relationships between the points you're making.

As for how to structure each of your main points, ideas, or arguments, here is a basic template to follow. It goes by the acronym "PEEL" (you can think of it as a way to "peel" away the different layers of an idea you're discussing or a point you are making). Here it is:

1. **Point.** State your point/idea/argument concisely in one sentence. A good example comes from Amy Cuddy's TED talk: "Your Body Language Shapes Who You Are" (See the TED talk here:

http://www.ted.com/talks/amy_cuddy_your_body_language_shapes_who_you_are/). When she starts discussing her second main idea, she says this (notice also that she signposts): "So the second question really was, you know, so we know that our minds change our bodies, but is it also true that our bodies change our minds?" That's it.

2. **Elaborate.** Obviously, a single sentence isn't enough to fully explore one of your main points. So dedicate another sentence (or two, or three) to delving into this point on a deeper level. You can mention or discuss any supporting ideas or subtopics—ideas that support your main point(s).

3. **Evidence.** Now you need to support your claim or point with evidence. This is where you bring up examples, facts, figures, statistics, stories, and any other evidence you want to share with your audience.

4. **Link.** Summarize your point, demonstrate that it supports your main idea and/or the purpose of your speech. Then, for a smooth transition, "link" it to the next point or idea you are going to discuss.

Now reading that structure probably makes you a little… bored. I'll be the first to admit it's not the most exciting thing in the world. However, it's just that: a structure. Here's how to make it a little more exciting and make sure your audience remembers what you've told them…

The Secret to Being Impossible to Forget

If you've listened to many speeches, there's probably a fair chunk of them where you can't remember a single thing they told you. You don't want this to be you. So here's how to ensure you make your message and points unforgettable…

The first key to having your audience remember what you've told them is to understand how people actually remember things. There are four stages:

1. **Hearing.** First, your audience must hear what it is you have to say. They're not going to remember it if they couldn't hear you.
2. **Attention.** Second, you must have their attention. We can only consciously focus on one thing at a time. If they're on their phone or daydreaming about their next vacation, they're not going to remember what you said.
3. **Understanding.** Third, they must understand what you're telling them. In high school, I *heard* my chemistry teacher speak. He even had my full *attention*. But I didn't understand most of it. So I didn't remember it. Simple enough.
4. **Remembering.** Finally, if your audience can hear you and you've got their attention and they understand the points you are making, they will be able to remember it. You can also help them remember your points with the techniques below…

Read below for some different ways you can grab your audience's attention, help them to understand a point you're making, and, of course, remember…

- **Humor.** Humor hits several birds with one stone. Humor grabs your audience's attention. Humor is memorable. And humor can also help your audience understand a point you're making.
- **Relevance.** How is what you're saying relevant to them? How can they apply it to their own life? How does what you're saying affect them?
- **Examples.** Examples help make your message easier to grasp.
- **Stories.** Us humans are hardwired to remember stories much, much, *much* better than standalone facts. Use this to your advantage by doing a bit of storytelling.

- **Visuals.** Do *not* make the mistake of using your PowerPoint as a crutch. It is not there for you to read off. It is not there for your audience to read off, either (they should be listening to you instead). Ideally, your presentation slides should either have only a few words (e.g. a *very* concise statement—your main point) or graphics (and they should likewise be very simple graphics, not distracting ones). Just look at a Steve Jobs presentation to see what I mean. Anyway, visuals—if used right—can definitely help your audience to remember and understand what you're saying. They can also help you retain everybody's attention.
- **Contrast.** "To be or not to be?" "Float like a butterfly, sting like a bee." "The best means of insuring peace is to be prepared for war." Compare and contrast your ideas. Contrast does a great job of yanking our attention. It also makes things very easy to understand, helping us to remember.
- **Repetition.** Repetition makes things much easier to remember. Martin Luther King's "I Have a Dream" speech is a great example of this. King repeated "I have a dream…" eight times in a row, expressing different ideas, hopes, and dreams. Obama is also a big fan of repetition. For example, during his 2004 keynote speech at the Democratic National Convention, Obama repeated many times, "There's not an [X] America and a [Y] America; there's a United States of America."

Moving on, let's take a look at how to finish your speech with impact and leave your audience wowed…

CONCLUSION: TELL THEM WHAT YOU TOLD THEM

You've given your speech. You seized your audience's attention from the get-go with a powerful introduction. You then discussed your main points in an engaging and interesting way, winning your audience over to your way of thinking.

Now what?

Now you need to finish your speech off with a bang. You need to end on a high note. Here's a basic template for finishing your speech:

1. **Restate your purpose.** Reiterate the message, lesson, or key things that you want your audience to remember.
2. **Summarize your main points.** Briefly restate each of your three (or however many) main points. In other words, "tell 'em what you told 'em."
3. **Your final statement.** Finish off with a broader statement, showing your audience how what you've told them relates to the big picture. You can also finish by referring back to your attention grabber at the very beginning of your speech. For example, remember how, in his TED talk, Dan Pink started off by "confessing" that he went to law school? Well, here's how he finished his speech: "I rest my case." You can finish off your speech in a similar fashion by going back to your initial attention grabber.

It's really that simple.

Restate the one big thing you want your audience to remember (the purpose of your speech).

Summarize your main points.

Return to your opening theme/attention grabber.

Done.

STORYTELLING

Telling a powerful story can be the difference between a speech that's just "okay" and a speech that's unforgettable. Furthermore, storytelling can be an excellent way to start your speech, grab your audience's attention, and introduce the theme or topic that you'll be talking to your audience about.

So then, how can you become a master storyteller and have your audience hanging on to your every word? Read on to find out…

The Secrets to Unforgettable Storytelling

Here are some different ways to ensure your story is engaging and captivating rather than boring and tedious:

- **Tailor your story to your audience.** When deciding upon a story to include in your speech, it is essential to keep your audience in mind. Storytelling can be a bit like humor: what is funny to one audience might not be funny to another. A story that you'd tell to a room of executives may be different than what would engage a room of college students, so make sure to keep your audience in mind.
- **Make sure your story has purpose.** Don't tell a story for the sake of telling a story. Your story *must* have purpose. It *must* link into the topic, theme, or objective of your speech. You must ask yourself, "What do I want my audience to get out of this story?" When it comes to storytelling, always start with the end in mind.

- **Make your story personal.** The best stories are ones that are personal. Your audience will be a whole lot more interested and engaged if it's something from your own life—an anecdote. Moreover, you can poke a little fun at yourself and expose your fears, habits, or mistakes. This lets the audience identify with you and be much more receptive to what you have to say.
- **Keep it short.** You don't want your audience to be wondering, "When the hell is this person going to finish this damn story already?!" If your story takes too long, it loses its impact. To keep it short…
- **Eliminate nonessential details.** Keep it short and snappy, sharing only the information that is necessary for the point you are making. If something doesn't add to your story, cut it out.
- **Practice makes perfect.** You will, of course, want to practice your entire speech—however you'll especially want to practice your storytelling skills so it comes out naturally and not as if you're just reading off a memorized script. You could also rehearse your story in front of a few friends and get their feedback.
- **Master your nonverbals.** Nonverbals are *especially* important when recounting an anecdote or telling a story. You can pause to build suspension, use gestures to demonstrate movement, emotion, location, shape, size, etc. You can do different voices for different characters. You can also use your voice (and body) to show excitement, sorrow, and other emotions relevant to your story.

3 STEPS TO BECOMING THE MOST CHARISMATIC PERSON IN THE ROOM

In her book *The Charisma Myth*, Olivia Fox Cabane claims that there are three components to charisma: warmth, power, and presence. Read on to learn more about each…

1. **Charisma Key #1: Warmth.** In other words, be friendly. Smile. Look approachable. Be nice. If you're an unapproachable jerk who alienates people, people are not going to consider you very charismatic.
2. **Charisma Key #2: Power.** My delivery lady is very friendly. She smiles, we make small talk whenever she delivers something, and she gives me a wave whenever I see her around. But… she's not very powerful. She's a delivery lady. She doesn't exactly have a presence that oozes of power and authority. While you don't need to be a world leader or billionaire CEO to meet this power requirement, you do need to develop an aura of power and authority. Your body language and other nonverbals are key to doing this.
3. **Charisma Key #3: Presence.** Bill Clinton is famous for his undeniable charisma. Even people who just shook his hand say that, for that split second, they felt as if it were only the two of them in existence. Everything else faded away. Bill Clinton was *completely* focused on them, and only them. In other words, he was fully present. Now imagine if Clinton was distracted by something else he was thinking about, off in his own little world. Or if he was simultaneously shooting off an email on his phone

while meeting and greeting people. All of a sudden, he loses that awesome charisma. He has warmth and power, but without presence, he loses that charisma. So that's the final key to charisma: being fully present.

Okay, so how do you apply these three keys to charisma to your public speaking endeavors?

Let's take another look at these three keys with different ways you can use each when speaking to an audience…

1. **Warmth.** Display warmth when speaking to an audience by using humor and telling personal stories. When you open up about yourself or make yourself a little vulnerable—such as by recounting a story when you made a funny mistake (that's relevant to your speech/audience)—you allow your audience to connect with you. You can also display warmth by smiling, talking in a friendly manner, and so on.
2. **Power.** Contrary to what you might have initially thought, you don't actually need to be powerful to be charismatic. You just need to have a powerful, authoritative aura. Refer back to the first section in this book on nonverbal communication to learn how to develop a powerful, authoritative, awe-inspiring presence.
3. **Presence.** You need to be fully present and focused on your audience. Don't look at your slides. Don't look at your notes. Don't look at your feet or your hands or the exit. Focus 100 percent on your audience and be completely present. Make solid eye contact with them. Also make sure you're fully focused on the moment and not thinking about something else in the back of your mind (or else your eyes will have that glazed over look of someone who's not really there, but off in la-la land).

HOW TO PREPARE TO GIVE THE SPEECH OF YOUR LIFE

Like any activity, when it comes to public speaking, practice makes perfect. Even the best of the best practice and practice and practice. Martin Luther King agonized for weeks and weeks over getting his "I Have a Dream" speech just perfect. Steve Jobs used to spend days and days and days repeatedly rehearsing his product presentations. Behind every great speech, there's a lot of preparation.

Read on to discover some simple steps for creating, refining, and perfecting your speech and it's delivery…

5 STEPS TO PREPARING THE PERFECT SPEECH

Here are five steps to preparing a great speech…

1. **Determine the purpose (and topic) of your speech.** Before you do anything else, you must know exactly what you hope to accomplish with this speech. Once you've determined the end you hope to achieve (the purpose of the speech), you need to decide on a topic and core message. For example, if your talk is on global warming, will your core message be to plant more trees? To invest in clean energy? To reduce your emissions? As you can see, the same topic can have many different core messages. Determine what your core message will be so you can frame the rest of your presentation around that.
2. **Outline your speech.** If your speech doesn't have structure, your

audience will get lost and your "speech" will be little more than a randomly assembled collection of incomplete thoughts. Once you've identified a topic and purpose (or core message) for your speech, start outlining your main supporting points. You can also start outlining your introduction (such as what attention grabber you might kick off speech with), supporting evidence, stories, examples, engaging points, and so on.

3. **Write your speech.** Now that you've determined the purpose of your speech and done a rough outline, it's time to start your first draft. Once you've fleshed out your outline into a rough draft, you'll want to interactively edit and refine your speech, moulding it into its most effective form. That said, if you're just giving a short, informal speech, you could stop at the outline level and wing it from there. However, if you're giving a more important or formal speech, or if the stakes are higher (or if you're getting paid to speak), you will almost certainly want to flesh it out in more detail, write it up, and practice, practice, practice so you can get used to the flow of your speech and memorize it.

4. **Add gestures, tonality, and visuals.** Public speaking is *not* public reading. You don't just print out your draft and read it off a piece of paper. Unfortunately, many people act as if they just need to read their speech from memory. But a speech is so much more. You need gestures. You need verbal expression. And in many cases, you'll need visuals. A speech isn't something to be read—it's not a book or an essay—a book is something to be listened and watched, like film or theatre. So practice your speech in front of a mirror or video camera and add gestures as well as vocal inflections and expressiveness. Keep in mind that gestures and vocal expression should come naturally—you don't want them to look and sound artificial or forced. Moreover, planning out gestures and tonality will confuse you and distract you from what you need to say. Instead, the best route is to practice your speech until gesturing and vocal expressiveness becomes natural.

5. **Practice and seek feedback.** Get a friend, spouse, one of your children, or anybody else and practice giving them your speech or presentation. Not only can they give you feedback, but simply practicing in front of somebody else will make you more aware of any wording or expressions that sound silly, awkward, or a bit odd. It will also help you to be a little bit less nervous. Even practicing in front of someone you know and love (such as a friend or family member) can make you a little nervous, which will help to prepare you a bit for speaking to a larger audience.

Now let's take a look at a simple guideline for creating a great presentation…

THE 10/20/30 FORMULA FOR THE PERFECT PRESENTATION

If your speech is going to be accompanied by a PowerPoint presentation, you'll want to read this section…

Far too many people make the mistake of having countless slides, filling those slides from top to bottom with walls of text in small font, and rambling on for a tediously long time.

Fortunately, there's a simple formula that can help you avoid all of these mistakes. Brainchild of the venture capitalist Guy Kawasaki (https://guykawasaki.com/), it's called "The 10/20/30 Rule of PowerPoint."

(Note: Once again, consider how this applies to your specific circumstances or purpose. This rule doesn't necessarily need to be followed to the letter. It is also worth noting that Kawasaki intended his "10/20/30 Rule" to be used by entrepreneurs pitching their startup to venture capitalists—not as a universal presentation template. That said, it undoubtedly serves as a great template for creating a great presentation.)

Here's how the 10/20/30 rule works:

1. **Ten slides.** Your audience won't be able to comprehend or remember more than ten concepts. Don't bombard them with several dozen slides. Keep it simple. Another advantage to this is that it means your audience will be fully focused on you and what you're saying rather than taking in a new slide every ten seconds.
2. **Twenty minutes.** Guy Kawasaki recommends entrepreneurs give their ten slides in twenty minutes, allowing the remaining 40 minutes (assuming it's an hour-long meeting) for people arriving late, leaving early, technical problems (such as the projector playing up) as well as answering questions and having a discussion. Consider how this compares to your situation and the purpose of your speech and adjust accordingly.
3. **Thirty-point font.** Don't make the mistake of having tiny font that nobody can read. You want your audience to be able to read what you've got on your slide. More than that, you don't want your slide filled with a wall of text in a tiny font. You want your audience to be listening to you, not reading off your slide.

Something else you'll also want to consider is the importance of visuals. Rather than just filling your PowerPoint slides with text, use visuals (such as a relevant image, illustration, diagram, graph, etc.) to help your audience comprehend your points.

Moving on, let's now take a look at some of the best ways to quickly and efficiently memorize your speech…

HOW TO QUICKLY AND EFFICIENTLY MEMORIZE YOUR SPEECH FROM START TO FINISH

Almost everybody is, on some level or another, petrified of public speaking. And much of this fear of public speaking stems from the fear that we will forget what we need to say and just freeze up in front of everybody.

Fortunately, there are ways you can help ensure you don't draw a blank and forget your speech in front of your audience.

When you're able to recall your speech from memory, you'll not only be noticeably more confident, but you'll also be able to maintain eye contact and overall be a more powerful and dynamic speaker. Your audience will also perceive you to be more knowledgeable and credible as well.

Read on for a few different ways of memorizing your speech...

Speech Memorization Technique #1: How to Memorize Your Speech Word for Word

The first step to memorizing your speech verbatim is to write out your speech in full. Then print it out and walk around your home (so you stay awake and alert) and read it out loud a few times. Then read out only the first sentence. Memorize it. Read out the first sentence from memory without looking at your printed text. Then do the same for the second sentence, until you have the first two sentences fully memorized. And so on, until you have memorized the first paragraph and can read it from memory. And on, and on, until your entire speech is memorized.

Once you can give your entire speech from memory (and have practice it a few times in this manner), go do something else for several hours. Then, later that day (or the next day), come back and see if you can still give your entire speech from memory. You will have most likely forgotten several parts of it, so repeat the process.

This technique can work for short speeches, however I would not recommend you use this technique for longer speeches. If you do, you may end up forgetting parts of your speech due to the stress of actually being in front of a real audience (as opposed to practicing in the comfort of your home).

Another downside is that, if you're not careful, you can come off as aloof and a bit distant (which your audience will feel) as you recite your memorized speech. You also run the risk of the speech sounding unnatural and too forced, as if you're reading off a piece of paper rather than having an naturally flowing conversation with the audience.

Speech Memorization Technique #2: Create a Memory Palace

Us humans are terrible at memorizing verbatim text. It can be done, but it's hard and typically only any good for short speeches.

If you need to give a longer speech, or if you want your speech to flow better and sound more natural, you're going to have to use a technique that works better with how your brain works. This is a technique used not only by many professional public speakers, but also by memory champions.

Instead of trying to remember verbatim text, you remember things that the brain has evolved to naturally be better at remembering: images, concepts, stories, and the relationships between ideas.

For example, if I asked you to remember a random phone number or remember that the granny across the road who used to bake delicious jam scones got run over by a purple Ferrari last weekend while at church... well, I think you get the idea. You're obviously going to have a much easier time remembering what happened to the granny. Your brain is just much better at remembering images and stories than it is at remembering isolated pieces of information.

You can use this to your advantage with the memory palace technique. Here's how it works:

1. **Create an in-depth outline for your speech.** Your attention grabber, your main points, any examples, stories, or evidence you'll need, and so on.
2. **Attach certain images to each part of your outline.** Make sure they are memorable images, such as a fluffy pink elephant sitting outside your home, or a big sumo wrestler bouncing on your bed, or a jug of frozen blood in your freezer. Also make sure that they are somehow related to each part of your outline, reminding you of what to speak about. You can also organize everything (in your mind) so that as you walk through your home (in your mind), your speech is in the right order.
3. **To give your speech, mentally walk through your home.** As you walk through your home, you'll see all of these bizarre things you've placed there, which will remind you of exactly what you need to talk about in each section of your speech. As you finish each section or paragraph of your speech, walk into the next room. And so on, until you've given your entire speech.

To give a crude example, let's say you're giving a speech about why you predict your consumer goods company will grow over the next year. Your three main points are:

1. **Lowered income tax** will result in more spending.
2. **Increasing wages** will result in more spending.
3. **Increasing consumer confidence** will result in increased spending.

You could remember these three points by creating in your mind an image of a bloodied axe wedged into a pallet of cash with a pink men's shirt hanging off the axe's handle.

The bloodied axe would remind you of "slashed" income tax rates, the pallet of cash would remind you of increasing wages, and the pink men's shirt would remind you of increasing consumer "confidence."

You'd have a much easier time remembering these three points by having that image in your mind than you would were you to try remember these points just by themselves.

You can then use this technique to remember much more information by—in your imagination—placing this axed palette of cash outside your front door. And as you go through your speech, you'd imagine yourself going into your home and walking through each room.

In each of your home's rooms would be another memorable image which would remind you of other parts of your speech.

For example, as you walk through your home and into your bedroom, there might be a big tiger (or panda) on your bed with a tranquilizing dart in it's back. This would remind you to speak about Asia's economic slowdown and how this will impact your company's profits.

You'd then continue moving on through your home (and speech). You might then walk into your garage and see President Trump has pulled a box of lego out of the cupboard and is building a lego wall. This would remind you to speak about how trade barriers and import tariffs might affect profits. As you look closer, you see President Trump is wearing reading glasses so he can accurately see his toy wall. This might remind you to speak about your company's glass imports will be impacted by policy changes. Trump then reaches into his suit pocket and pulls out a toy kangaroo, which he proceeds to bounce along the top of his lego wall. This would remind you to mention how business is going in Australia. And so on.

Although I've given a terribly crude example, hopefully you can see the power of this technique and how it can make memorizing your speeches so much easier.

In sum, you simply have to outline your speech with all the details you need to cover and then create a "memory palace," such as in the example above. Do this, and you'll be able to memorize an entire speech in no time.

Speech Memorization Technique #3: Put Your Speech in Dot Point Form

This is my favorite technique if I'm giving a presentation that isn't too long and that's on a subject I'm very familiar with. (My second favorite technique is the memory palace technique described above.)

This is also the easiest technique.

It works like this:

1. **Create a speech outline.** Outline all your major points, as well as any examples, stories, evidence, attention grabbers, etc. you're going to use. Make sure to give your outline good structure.

2. **Create a presentation using PowerPoint.** Or Apple Keynote. Or Google Slides. Or whatever you use. Make sure to not fill your slides with text. Stick as closely to Guy Kawasaki's 10/20/30 Rule as you can. Just have *very* concise dot points and/or relevant visuals.
3. **Rehearse your presentation a few times.** Yeah seriously, that's it. Deploy your attention grabber, tell your audience the main points you'll be talking to them about, and let them know what the purpose (or core message) of your speech is. Then discuss your main points one at a time, casually glancing at your PowerPoint slide each time you change slides and/or if you get lost or have your mind go blank.

If you're just giving a speech (and not a presentation), you can still use this same technique. Just get a sticky note, palm card, or small piece of paper and jot down your main points and subpoints. As you go through your speech, you can refer back to this if you ever get lost or have a moment of forgetfulness.

In sum, this technique is more casual, relaxed, and conversational. This can be a good thing, as your speech will flow very naturally and your audience will be engaged by your relaxed, conversational manner. However, this can also be a bad thing if the speech you're giving is supposed to be very formal or if this is not the impression you want to give. So consider these factors (as well as other factors, such as who your audience is, etc.) when determining whether or not to use this technique in a specific situation.

CONCLUSION

Public speaking is an unavoidable part of many careers. Whether it be pitching investors, winning over clients, swaying superiors, inspiring and educating an audience, or any of the other numerous ways in which it can be utilized, public speaking can be a scary and uncertain endeavor.

On the flip side, mastering the ability to speak to and engage an audience can yield great dividends. If you're an entrepreneur, it can lead to investors flocking to fund your startup. If you run or work in a client-based business, it can help you land big clients. If you're an author or researcher, it can lead to you getting lots of paid speaking engagements. If you're a corporate employee, it can increase your influence within your organization, make you appear highly credible, and even lead to you more quickly climbing through the ranks. Whatever your profession, public speaking can prove to be an invaluable skill.

By mastering nonverbal communication—including your body language, hand gestures, and tone of voice—you can develop an aura of power and authority. (Or so-called "executive presence," which one study found accounts for 26 percent of the decision on whether or not to promote someone.)

By understanding how to incorporate "ethos", "pathos", and "logos" into your rhetoric, you can more easily sway and influence.

By learning how to structure a speech—from your attention grabber and introduction, to your main points and conclusion—you can quickly organize your thoughts into a remarkably coherent framework and deliver a speech that captivates from the get-go.

By becoming a skilled storyteller, you can rapidly earn your audience's rapt attention and drive home your core message in a way that will be simply unforgettable.

By cultivating undeniable charisma, you can make others perceive you as highly credible and competent and give yourself the advantage of having the "halo effect" on your side.

By being able to creating simple yet powerful presentations and speak to your audience from memory, you give yourself the advantage of being able to engage with your audience on a whole new level and win them over to your way of thinking with unparalleled ease.

As you learned at the beginning of this book, so-called "human engineering"—your ability to communicate, negotiate, and lead—accounts for 85 percent of your financial success. As such, public speaking—a crucial component of "human engineering"—can either hold your down or lift your up. Hopefully after reading this book, it will be the latter.

Printed in Great Britain
by Amazon